Wonders of the Hive

DODD, MEAD WONDER BOOKS

Wonders of the Seashore by Jacquelyn Berrill

Wonders of the Woodland Animals by Jacquelyn Berrill

Strange Nurseries by Jacquelyn Berrill

Wonders of the Wild by Jacquelyn Berrill

Wonders of the Antarctic by Jacquelyn Berrill

Wonders of the Tree World by Margaret Cosgrove

Wonders of Your Senses by Margaret Cosgrove

The Wonders Inside You by Margaret Cosgrove

Wonders of the Bird World by Helen Gere Cruickshank

Wonders of the Heavens by Kenneth Heuer

Wonders of the Aquarium by Sigmund A. Lavine

Wonders of the Hive by Sigmund A. Lavine

*Wonders of the Ocean Zoo by Boris Arnov, Jr.,
and Helen Mather-Smith Mindlin*

Wonders of the Hive

by Sigmund A. Lavine

ILLUSTRATED WITH PHOTOGRAPHS

DODD, MEAD & COMPANY
New York 1958

Library of Congress Catalog Card Number: 58-6452
Printed in the United States of America

For Dad—

who unlike honeybees sees all flowers as blue

Acknowledgments

If an actual count were taken of those who have helped to make this book possible, the total would be thousands. Most of them are nameless — for they are the residents of my hives whose daily activities have taught me much. However, there are five individuals who do have names and I would be most ungrateful not to mention them. Therefore, I wish to thank Earl Leighton, good neighbor and friend, who helped me set up my first hive; John A. Root of the A. I. Root Company, who furnished much useful material; Professor F. R. Shaw of the University of Massachusetts, who suggested picture sources; and Professor M. V. Smith of the Department of Apiculture in Ontario Agriculture College, Guelph, Ontario, who provided many of the illustrations. A special word of appreciation is due James I. Hambleton, Director of Bee Culture Research for the United States Department of Agriculture, for, despite the tremendous pressure of his schedule, he found time to read my manuscript with a scientific eye and thus assure that, while it may not be as perfect as a bee's cell, it is accurately constructed.

SIGMUND A. LAVINE

Contents

Wonders of the Hive

"The Pedigree of Honey . . ."

Until man developed methods of extracting sugar from cane and beet in comparatively recent times, his desire for something sweet could be satisfied only by honey. At first, like the cavemen in the rock paintings on the walls of a prehistoric dwelling near Valencia in Spain, he "robbed" the nests of wild bees – but as the years passed, he learned that a rude hive was a far more satisfactory source of the bee's golden treasure. However, despite this early association of men and bees, it wasn't until about two hundred

Photograph courtesy Ontario Agricultural College

While seeking pollen and nectar, honeybees unwittingly cross-pollinate vegetation. Were it not for this, many plants would not develop seeds or fruit and man would starve.

years ago that scientists interested in the residents of the hive learned to appreciate their importance to mankind – not only as manufacturers of honey, but as pollinators. To their amazement, they found that few believed their reports – so great was the mass of myths, legends, superstitions and folklore dealing with bees and honey that had accumulated over the centuries.

Even great-grandmother's doctor paid little attention to these pioneer entomologists (as students of insect life are called) but continued to prescribe honey for various illnesses, as did the medical men who practiced in the days when the tyrants of Egypt were building the mighty pyramids. Yet it is doubtful that any of these ancient physicians had more faith in the curative power of honey than the New Hampshire doctor who suggested the following mixture to those who wished to rid themselves of freckles:

half a pound of honey	2 oz. glycerine
2 oz. alcohol	6 drops citric acid

Perhaps you prefer to eat honey on hot biscuits to spreading it on your face in hope of removing skin blemishes. But don't laugh at this formula – many present-day manufacturers of cosmetics use honey in cold cream, hand lotion and salve, while an English firm recently introduced a new lipstick made from solidified honey colored with rust! So scholars examining the ancient books of Persia, India and China are not surprised to find many references to honey as a medicine and a beauty aid.

These yellowed scrolls of parchment tell many other facts about bees, honey and beekeeping in ancient times. So does the cuneiform writing on the cylinder-shaped clay tablets of Babylonia, while a brittle papyrus from Egypt discloses the first known use of a bee as a symbol – a hieroglyph representing royalty. In all of these countries, honey played an important part in religious ceremonies and beeswax was used to make a wide variety of items ranging from sorcerer's demons to molds for the casting of bronze statues.

While there is no way of telling when the Hebrews began to keep bees, it must have been at a very early period of their history, for the Old Testament and the Talmud contain many references to them. Perhaps the best known is the description of Canaan as a land "flowing with milk and honey." Elsewhere, we are told that the judgments of the Lord are "sweeter than honey and the honeycomb" and His works are "sweeter than honey to my mouth." Because the Hebrews believed in only one God, unlike most ancient peoples, they have no myths about bees nor did they ever believe that they were divine creatures. However, in times of joy or sorrow, they always give honey as a gift, because they feel it adds to happiness and overcomes bitterness.

Although little is known of the beekeeping practices of the Arabian neighbors of the Hebrews, the Koran, or Scripture of Mohammedanism, includes a book entitled, *Sura* or *The Bee*. Its passages show that the desert folk honored the hard-working insect, considered honey a delicious food and esteemed it as medicine. In the Middle Ages – a period when Arab culture was the finest in the world – many Arabic authors wrote books about the habits of bees and their value to man. Probably most of their material came from the Greeks, with whom they had many contacts in the first centuries following the birth of Christ.

They couldn't have had better teachers, for, long before blind Homer wrote the *Iliad* and the *Odyssey*, his countrymen feasted on honey. At first, like all peoples, the Greeks knew only the sweetness stolen from wild bees, but by degrees beekeeping became such an important industry that Aristophanes, writing about 400 B.C., mentions honey and wax merchants. During the same period, Hippocrates, father of medicine and author of the oath every doctor takes on the day he receives his degree, was prescribing honey for many ills. Hippocrates had no fear that the honey his patients ate might be impure – the great lawmaker of Athens, Solon, had included regulations governing beekeeping when he set down his famous code. Only one scientific study dealing with bees written during this period has come down to us — the work of Aristotle, tutor and friend of Alexander the Great. While much of what he wrote was not true, his statements dominated the thinking of men for hundreds of years.

The average Greek, however, paid little attention to laws or scholarly works dealing with bees and honey. He enjoyed its sweetness, made it into a drink long before he had wine and used beeswax for sealing letters, making models, or protecting metals from the weather. But he always shared the treasure of the hive with his gods — either when he wanted a favor, or wished to thank them — for, according to legend, Zeus, king of all the gods, was hidden in a cave to protect him from his angry father when he was a baby. Here he was fed and protected by bees. Greeks also offered honey to the dwellers on Olympus because they believed that the gods drank only nectar and ate nothing but ambrosia. Nectar is the sweet juice bees sip out of flowers, while ambrosia is a mixture of honey and milk. Incidentally, this diet was supposed to make the gods immortal and it was the duty of Hebe, wife of Hercules and goddess of youth, to serve it at mealtime.

There are countless references to bees and honey in Greek mythology and one of the most delightful explains why some men are gifted with beautiful singing voices, others can sway an audience when they deliver a speech, and still others have the ability to write poetry. According to the ancient tale, the reason is that the Muses, goddesses of the arts and sciences, order a bee to place a drop of honey on the lips of these fortunate individuals shortly after they are born.

Apiculture, or the raising of bees, was probably introduced into Italy by Greek or Phoenician settlers and by the time Rome's mighty legions had conquered the known world, beekeeping was a most important part of Roman agriculture. The various activities of the hive attracted the attention of many of the authors whose works are read today as part of every high-school course in Latin literature. Most charming of all these accounts is that written by Virgil, the greatest Roman poet, who added to his income by selling honey and wax. You will find it in the *Georgics,* a long poem that describes the joys of country life and the pleasures of being close to nature.

No man in the long history of beekeeping loved the honey makers more than Virgil and, if legend is true, they repaid his constant attention when a passing band of plundering soldiers attempted to rob him. Before the intruders were able to steal his possessions, the poet's faithful servants hid everything of value among the hives. They then told the bees what was happening and the insects swarmed out in an angry cloud and stung the invaders so severely that they fled in terror!

Honey played an important part in Roman religious life, as it did in that of Greece, for soothsayers claimed they could predict the future by observing the actions of swarming bees. More honey was used in cooking than was eaten in the comb and one Latin author wrote, "The baker can deliver sweet foods to you in a thousand forms, for the bee works for him." Various drinks were made of honey and many of them were considered excellent medicines – the Roman formula for reaching a ripe old age being *Oleo externus, internus melle,* which means "oil externally, honey internally."

Bleached beeswax was used by Roman sculptors to cover any defects in their work – but master craftsmen, proud that their handiwork was perfect, signed statements that their statues were *sine cera,* "without wax." This is the origin of our expression "Yours sincerely."

The names of many places in Central Europe derived from *Bienen* and *Immen,* meaning bees, and from *seideln,* "to collect honey," is proof that beekeeping is an ancient art in the region that comprises modern-day Germany, Czechoslovakia, Switzerland and the Slavic countries. It began when primitive tribesmen settle down in villages and kept crude log hives and used the honey to make mead – the drink tradition says was served to the mighty warriors in the halls of Valhalla. When worship of Odin and the other gods of Asgard gave way to Christianity, apiculture was encouraged, for the Catholic Church used – as if still does – a tremendous number of wax candles. In order to supply these, many monasteries engaged in beekeeping, or collected the rents due them in wax.

It was during this period that churchmen, wishing to teach morality, compared the life of bees with that of Christ and suggested that man might well copy the industrious life of the hive. Meanwhile, religious artists were using the bee as a symbol in their paintings. A common subject was St. Ambrose with a beehive in the background – based on the legend that when he was a baby, his lips had been smeared with honey. The most famous of these pictures hangs behind the high altar of the church named for him in Milan, Italy, which shows bees swarming about Ambrose in his cradle. Another example of the use of the bee in medieval art is found in a picture by Titian, the great Venetian master – it shows the Infant Jesus with a bee in his hand.

Feudal lords demanded payments of wax and honey from their serfs and enforced strict regulations governing the building of hives, the tapping of wild bees' nests, the sale of honey and other such matters. These codes also stated the rights of beekeepers. However, these privileges were often ignored when a walled city was besieged and hot water and rocks failed to keep the enemy from raising scaling ladders. Then, the defenders threw beehives on the invaders, who usually fled in terror! Incidentally, this technique was used in Africa during the First World War, when German troops "bombed" British soldiers with bees.

Little was written about the honey makers during the Middle Ages. The few facts and many fictitious statements set down by Greek and Roman authors were accepted without question – and both nobles and commoners alike believed bees had supernatural powers. As a result, the insects were asked to drive away evil spirits, to make fields fertile and to protect their owners. Honey also played an important part in wedding ceremonies –

Photograph by Wide World

Bees entered this quaint twelfth century German hive through the hole in the lady's skirt.

the old Germanic custom of drinking mead for a month after a marriage is the source of our "honeymoon."

As industry and commerce became more important in Europe than agriculture, hard-headed traders and skilled members of the guilds, located in the towns, cast aside the age-old beliefs in the magical powers of bees and the sorcery of honey. But in the country, the ancient customs survived—as they still do. Moreover, so firmly had the bee become established as a symbol of industry and royalty that Napoleon covered his coronation robes with golden bees and had them woven into his flag. He was inspired to do this by the finding of 300 golden bees in the tomb of Childeric, the father of Clovis, whose conversion to Christianity you may have read about in history class. Some historians also claim that the French *fleur-de-lis* is not a lily, but a bee. The Little Corporal also used a bee in his coat-of-arms – a pun on the first letter of his last name, Bonaparte.

If you open up the telephone book of any large city, you will find such names as Beeman, Hives, Honey, Honeycut and Honeywell. The chances are that the ancestors of these people were English and kept bees, as did so many inhabitants of the British Isles – for sugar was not introduced into England until the fif-

Photograph courtesy Ontario Agricultural College

A sure sign of spring – a honeybee pollinator at work.

teenth century. Both rich and poor relied upon honey for sweetening and they also made it into medicine and beverages, while the nobles used wax candles for light and for measuring time. At first, the Britishers tapped the nests of wild bees. A law passed two years after the Magna Charta reads: "Every freeman . . . shall likewise have the honey found in his woods." As a matter of fact, nearly every ruler passed regulations governing the sale of honey and the purity of beeswax. In 1580, Queen Elizabeth signed an "Acte for the true melting, making and working of Waxe."

This royal interest in wax and honey prompted many authors to write books comparing the "perfect monarchie" of the hive to that of England, in hopes of being rewarded for their flattery. But far more important than these volumes, interesting as they are, were those observations set down by learned men who wanted no reward except the satisfaction of adding to the world's knowledge, so, instead of blindly accepting the reports of early writers, they began to study bees scientifically. Their investigations have added much to the understanding of residents of the hive.

However, practical manuals on bee-management did not wipe out legend and superstition. In fact, the hardy pioneers who sought religious and political freedom in America brought all the ancient beliefs with them. They soon discovered there were no native bees in the colonies and sent home for hives — the first shipment landing in 1638. The honey makers were called "white men's flies" by the Indians, who knew nothing of the sweetness of honey until escaping swarms nested in the woods — although South American tribes were beekeepers long before the Spaniards conquered their lands.

A story is told of an Indian who visited Danvers, Massachusetts, in 1640, and saw a horse being ridden, an ox ploughing a field and a farmer removing honeycomb from a hive. After watching for a few minutes, the Redman grunted, "White man work horse, white man work ox, white man work fly — this Indian go away!"

One of the most widespread customs that was carried across the Atlantic was telling the bees of a death in the family. Probably you have read Whittier's *Telling The Bees,* which describes draping each hive with black crepe at such a time. American beemen also chanted a rhyme so old that no one has been able to trace its origin:

A swarm of bees in May,
Is worth a load of hay;
A swarm of bees in June,
Is worth a silver spoon;
A swarm in July,
Is not worth a fly.

New England farmers still quote the above lines — because the earlier bees swarm, the sooner they will begin to store surplus honey for man's use.

American-English is full of phrases using the word bee. Among the most common are the "husking bee" of the frontier and the "spelling bee" of the little red schoolhouse. Another common expression is to say that anyone with a fixed idea has "a bee in his bonnet."

The only instance where a bee plays an important part in the religion of a civilized people is found in America. The Mormons use it as a symbol and their sacred writings, *The Book of Mormon,* tells how the bee, or "deseret" was carried into the Valley of Nimrod. Because of the high regard in which they held the bee and the great number of Mormons in Utah, it is not surprising that, when a name had to be chosen for that state when it entered the Union in 1896, Deseret was suggested. Although this honor was not given the bee, the great seal of Utah has a beehive in the center, surrounded by flowers and topped with the word, "Industry." Incidentally, Utah's nickname is "The Beehive State."

A modern supermarket, its shelves piled high with glass jars of honey, is a long journey in time and distance from a prehistoric Spanish cave, but all along the way man has enjoyed the sweetness of the hive. It would seem that the centuries-old association of man and bee leaves nothing still to learn about the honey makers. However, in laboratories and on experimental farms, trained scientists are studying bees and trying to blend their modern techniques with time-tested knowledge in order to improve the art of apiculture and insure that man will always enjoy honey, nature's sweetest gift.

Photograph by U.S.D.A.

Commercial beekeepers inspecting hives arranged alongside of blossoming cotton.

What Is a Bee?

Although ten thousand species of bees are known to man and new ones are being discovered and named every year, it isn't as easy to recognize a bee as you might think. Many two-winged flies resemble them a good deal in form and color, but you can spot the difference quickly, if you remember that a bee has four wings. However, among the thousands of kinds of bees there are a few that look so much like wasps that the only way they can be positively identified is by placing a specimen under a microscope or powerful magnifying glass. It is the hair that distinguishes them – for, although wasps appear to be bald, they are covered with a smooth "fur coat," while the thick hair that covers bees will be either barbed, branched, or feathery.

Bees belong to the largest group of animals in the world – known commonly as insects and scientifically as *Hexapoda.* Both names are most descriptive, for insect comes from the Latin "in sections" and *Hexapoda* is derived from the Greek *hex* (six) and *poda* (feet). The six-legged body of the true insect, such as a bee, is separated into three segmented sections: the head; the thorax, or middle part; and the abdomen. Therefore many "bugs" are not insects at all. Spiders, for example, have but two divisions to their body – a thorax bearing eight legs and an unsegmented abdomen.

Insects are found everywhere, living contentedly in the frigid cold of the polar regions, the torrid heat of the tropic jungles and the mild climate of the temperate zone. No one knows how many species exist. The total is estimated in the millions and scientists have described the life histories of some 300,000 different kinds.

Photograph by U.S.D.A.
Like all true insects the body of a bee is divided into three sections.

In order to classify this huge number of creatures, entomologists, like all naturalists, use a complicated "filing system." It places all the insects with the same physical appearance in large groups called "orders." Bees are members of the order *Hymenoptera,* a most descriptive word derived from the Greek *hymen* (membrane) and *pteron* (wing). However, the various species vary greatly. If bees were only as big as birds, it would be a simple task to distinguish between the different kinds. But, despite the fact that bees, like humans, vary in size, shape and color, the features that set one variety off from another can only be seen under a strong lens.

No matter what the color and pattern of their hairy coat, bees are divided into two major groups. The first consists of "social bees" – so-called because they form communities, work together to design living quarters, join in collecting and storing food and share the task of feeding and rearing their brood, or young. Most important of all bees in this classification is the *Apis mellifera*, the honeybee, which shares its golden treasure with man. Its scientific name comes from the Latin, *Apis* meaning "bee" and *mellifera* or "honey-bearer."

There are far more species in the second group, none of which live in hives – which is the case with most bees. A single female, without help, builds a nest for her brood, storing within its walls enough food to provide for the young until they are able to forage for themselves. Because of this characteristic the members of the second group are known as "solitary bees."

Solitary

Solitary Bees

Long before humans learned to bore a hole in wood, to mold clay into adobe, to plaster a wall, or to mine deep beneath the surface of the earth, solitary bees had mastered these skills – and they are still practicing them today, just as their ancestors did thousands of years ago.

While glass-walled hives make the observation of social bees relatively simple, solitary bees must be studied in the field. This calls for keen eyes and unlimited patience – but it is an engrossing experience for both trained naturalists and amateurs. In fact, Charles Ferton, a French entomologist and professional soldier, actually refused promotion so he could remain at his post in Corsica and continue his study of these insect artisans. But you don't have to travel to Napoleon's homeland to see the solitary bees at work. It is entirely possible that one of these clever craftsmen has a workshop in your back yard.

There are many varieties of carpenter bees, ranging in size from species a quarter of an inch in length to the tropic-dwelling *Xylocopa* – a very large insect whose name means "wood cutter" in Greek. But large or small, with no tools except their jaws, carpenter bees drill holes in and chisel out wood with as much precision as any human workman using steel tools – some kinds excavating wooden beams, others tunnelling in plant stems, in order to make their nests. But all of them raise their families the same way.

Photograph courtesy American Museum of Natural History

Carpenter bees on decayed twig lined with their "apartment-house" nurseries.

One of the most attractive of the carpenter bees is the tiny *Ceratina dupla*, with its metallic blue body and rainbow tinted wings. *Ceratina* means "small horned woman" in Greek (the horns being the antennae), while *dupla* is the Latin word for double. This species always selects a broken twig with a soft pith or center for a nesting site, preferring a sumac, elder, or raspberry bush. Starting at the break, mother bee digs out the pith, mouthful by mouthful, until she has a tunnel several inches long. When her work is as smooth as if it had been sandpapered, she places a mixture of pollen and nectar on the bottom of the excavation and lays a tiny white egg upon it.

Then, using pith chips glued together with saliva, the female erects a partition, fastening it to the sides of the gallery, thus forming a ceiling for the lowest nursery and a floor for the next one. In this fashion, the nest is filled with as many as fourteen one-room apartments, each containing a single egg and enough food for the baby bee that will hatch from it. A "vestibule" is always left near the opening, where the mother lives until her family is full-grown.

When the egg hatches, the young bee gorges itself on the "bee-bread," as the nectar-pollen paste left on the nursery floor is called. As is to be expected, the egg in the bottom cell hatches first, releasing a bee that reaches maturity long before its younger brothers and sisters. But it cannot get out because the tunnel is blocked. So it tears down the partition that separates its nursery from the one above, kicking the pieces behind it, and then waits patiently until the other members of the family go through the same process in turn. In time, all the pith is at the bottom of the nest and the young bees, their heads pointed toward the door, are free to fly into the world of flowers.

LEAF-CUTTER BEES

Known scientifically as *Megachile* ("big lips" in Greek) leaf-cutters are called a long list of harsh names by gardeners, for, although these insects which number hundreds of different kinds will use the foliage and petals of various plants and flowers to make their cells, our commonest species are fondest of rose leaves – a preference that makes them most unpopular!

Before foraging for leaves, the female looks for a tunnel to use for a nest – some leaf-cutters make their own in rotten wood or burrow in sandy soil, others use the space between warped shingles or holes in a wall, while still others "sub-let" the abandoned homes of boring insects. Having found a suitable apartment, mother leaf-cutter flies to a rose bush, straddles a leaf and, using her jaws like scissors, quickly snips out a large slice which she carries back to the nest. Wasting no time, she goes back for

Photograph courtesy American Museum of Natural History
Leaf-cutter bees are easily recognized by their scissors-like jaws.

more leaf pieces, fastening them together with saliva glue so that they overlap, completely lining the walls.

When her plastering is finished, the bee cuts a much smaller section out of a leaf and places it on the bottom of the nest cavity, pounding it into a wad on which she places a lump of bee-bread. Then she lays a single egg and covers it with a round segment of leaf, which becomes the base for the next cell. She repeats the routine until the burrow or tunnel is filled with thimble-like baskets in which she has placed her eggs. Finally, she cuts a leaf much larger than the rim of the nest and pushes it down so that it fits tightly. Sometimes one lid does not satisfy the anxious mother and she caps her nest with several leaves, in order to make sure the babies will be protected until they gnaw their way to freedom.

MASON BEES

Using either vegetable or mineral material moistened with saliva for mortar, mason bees, the cleverest of nature's construction crews, show a wide variation in nesting habits. There are many different kinds of these cement workers, with building techniques as varied as their choice in nesting sites – burrows deserted by other insects, the face of a large stone, or empty snail shells. Certain species prepare but one cell and lay but a single egg; others plaster ten to twenty cells and deposit an egg in each. Some varieties take great pains to conceal their nests – particularly those who use snail shells; still others make no attempt to hide them. Thus it is no wonder that Jean Henri Fabre, the French school-teacher, who devoted most of his small salary and all of his adult years to the study of insects, was fascinated by mason bees and wrote a book about them.

No mason bee is more skilled than *Chalicodoma muraria,* whose name, a combination of Latin and Greek, means "one that builds its home on stone." Confident that its cement will withstand attack by weather and natural enemies, it boldly chooses the face of a rock for a nesting site. Then, chewing soil until it is a soft, easily-worked lump, the female "trowels" the cells with her jaws, placing small pebbles in the outside walls to give added support – just as human masons add stone to strengthen concrete. But there is no roughness inside the cells – mother bee, fearful that her babies might injure themselves, smooths the walls with a coating of special mortar. As each upright cell is finished, a small amount of pollen and a glob of thick honey is placed on the floor, forming a cushion for an egg. Making more cement, the female covers all the cells with clay until she has a dome-shaped mass that resembles half an orange – a strong stone castle in which her children grow to maturity. Often several females build their nests close together, asking and giving no help until the nurseries are sealed. Then they work as a group, covering all the nests with a protective coat of thick mortar.

There is no comparison between the great depths man has reached in his search for valuable ore beneath the earth's surface and the six feet a mining bee burrows into the ground or side of a bank – but humans use machinery to sink their shafts, while the insect works with nothing but its jaws.

Scientists have classified nearly a thousand species of mining bees. Some merely dig a hole in the ground, pile the soil in a mound around the opening and line the excavation with cells containing one egg and enough bee-bread to last the baby until it can find its own food. Each cell is sealed off from the rest with a plug of saliva-moistened soil. Other miners display great engineering skill, boring a main tunnel out of which many short ones open. Here they lay their eggs. These "diggings" are protected from cave-ins by a glaze-like secretion which the female paints on the walls – corresponding to the timbers that support man-made shafts.

Although miners, like all solitary bees, build their cells alone, hundreds often choose the same bank for a nesting site, using a common entrance to the subterranean chambers. When the babies mature, the females, like good daughters, help mother with the housework, cleaning away waste material in the main hallway and side passages. Then they begin to raise their own families, flying in and out of the same doorway, but making their own cells, in which they place eggs and bee-bread without paying the slightest attention to their sisters.

Social Bees

Social bees are divided into three groups: *Bombidae,* or bumblebees; *Meliponidae,* or stingless bees; and *Apidae,* or hive bees.

Photograph courtesy Ontario Agricultural College

A group of thirsty honeybees gathering water from a pool.

The scientific name of the bumblebee is most appropriate, for it means buzzing in Greek – something they do loudly when their nest is disturbed! *Meliponidae* is also derived from the Greek. It comes from the words "honey" and "to work" and can be translated into "the honey gatherers." As you know, *Apis* means bee in Latin – the "ae" ending is the plural form.

Found all over the world, social bees range from hardy creatures capable of withstanding the cold blasts of the Arctic winds to the oases-dwellers of the Sahara Desert – said to be the best tempered of all. Smallest among them is a stingless species that lives in tropic jungles, the largest is the East Indian honeybee – but all of them, unlike their relatives the solitary bees, live in colonies and cooperate with each other for the common good.

While every solitary bee is either a male or an egg-laying female, a community of social bees includes a third member called a worker. The correct name for the mother bee is queen, that of the male, drone. Social bees differ from the solitary species in another way – they are the only bees that build nests from wax. Honeybees are greatly dependent upon this substance –

bumblebees make the least use of it — while stingless bees have a tendency to mix other sticky materials gathered during their foraging with the pure wax produced in their bodies.

Like the rungs of a ladder, each group of social bees marks a step upward in the development of the hive — first, the simple nest of the bumblebee, second the more complex structure of the stingless varieties; and finally, the complicated "city" of the honeybee. The degree of cooperation among the members of each of these groups varies in the same ratio as the skill displayed in building the nest. Let's take one step up the ladder and examine the life of the velvet-coated bumblebee.

BUMBLEBEES

Because bumblebees have such long tongues, thousands of them were shipped from England to Australia and New Zealand in 1855!

Perhaps vessels have carried stranger cargoes, but none more important — for the arrival of this one insured lush crops of the red clover planted "Down Under," to provide pasturage for the sheep herds. No other bee can reach inside the tiny florets of red clover and suck out nectar — the sweet secretion found at the base of flowers from which bees make honey. As the insects drink, grains of pollen, that magic golden dust that is the source of all seeds and fruit, sticks to their furry bodies and is carried to the next bloom they visit. This transfer of pollen from one plant to another is called pollination and it is of tremendous value to man — for unless it took place, we should have no fruit or vegetables. Incidentally, although honeybees are unable to gather nectar from red clover, they find it an excellent source of pollen and when collecting it are as effective in pollination as bumblebees.

Remarkable as it may seem, a foraging bee always visits flowers of the same species while gathering nectar — thus carrying

Photograph courtesy American Museum of Natural History

Farmers have no more helpful friend than the colorful and noisy bumblebee.

pollen where it is needed. However, not all pollination is the work of bees — wind, rain, birds and various crawling and flying insects also spread the golden dust. Sometimes humans resort to pollinating by hand — using powder puffs or delicate paint brushes, or shooting the pollen from one blossoming tree onto another with a shotgun. But no method devised by man is as effective as the plant world's best friend, the bee.

The story of the bumblebee, like that of many of Nature's children, begins in the spring. Awaking from hibernation —the deep sleep of winter — a young queen crawls out of her resting place, enjoys the warm sunshine for a week or two, then seeks a nesting site. Most of the 300 known species of bumblebees prefer to rear their family underground, in a deserted mouse, mole, or chipmunk nest, although some build on the surface — usually among grass roots.

Once a suitable burrow is found, the dried leaves used by the former inhabitants as bedding are piled into a mound, with a small hollow in the center. The female places a lump of bee-bread in this cavity and surrounds it with a wax cell the size of a pea, in which about a dozen eggs are laid. Unlike the young of other bees, these babies do not enjoy separate rooms — they share a common nursery. As they grow, the walls of the cells crack and the anxious mother patches them with additional wax. Bumblebees are devoted parents, laboriously feeding their children a partially digested liquid mixture of honey and pollen by sticking their long tongues through a gap in the top of the cell. At first the food is served "family style," but as the infants develop, they are fed individually. The most remarkable thing about mother bumblebee, though, is the fact that all the time her youngsters are growing up, she sits on the cell, just as a hen does when hatching and caring for chicks!

If you examine a bumblebee's nest, you'll find an open-mouthed wax cell about the size and shape of a marble near the entrance. Called a "honeypot," it is used to store the honey on which the female will feed at night and during wet weather. This emergency ration is constantly being eaten and replaced — for without honey, the bee cannot produce the body warmth necessary to rear her young. It is no easy task to keep the honeypot full and the babies warm at the same time, but she manages it. However, soon the mother has many willing helpers, for all of her first brood are workers, who, when fully developed, take over the duties of collecting nectar and pollen for bee-bread, patching the bulging cells of their younger brothers and sisters and building and filling honeypots.

Relieved of these chores, the queen never leaves the nest and does nothing but lay eggs. All during the summer months, only workers emerge from the cells, but with the approach of fall, young queens and drones appear. The males leave as soon as they are grown, but the females remain at home for a while. They do no work, however. Then they, too, take wing, leaving behind an exhausted mother and worn-out sisters who will soon die. Shortly thereafter, the young queens meet their mates (who live but three weeks), seek a snug burrow in which to hibernate, then sleep soundly until the sun's rays awake them the following spring, when they write a new chapter in the age-old story of the bumblebee.

STINGLESS BEES

Despite their name, these natives of the tropic regions of both the Old and New Worlds have a sting — but it is feeble and has no value as a defensive weapon. Some of the 250 species known to science are among the most gentle of bees and deserve their nickname *angelitos* or "little angels," while others have disagreeable dispositions, particularly the "hair twisters" of South America. When disturbed, they crawl into the ears, eyes and nose of the intruder, burrow under his clothing and entangle themselves in their victim's hair, constantly nipping with their jaws.

The nesting habits of stingless bees are as varied as their

Photograph by U.S.D.A.

A view of the interior of a nest of stingless bees from Brazil.

temperaments. They may suspend their homes from tree limbs, settle down in hollow trees, holes in the ground, or even in an ant hill! While some species make well-defined cells to hold their eggs, others lay them in clusters. Certain varieties build all cells the same size, others make those in which queens will be raised much larger than the rest. Some members of this family store honey and pollen in cells, but close relatives keep their food in wax jars. These differences in home building and cell making techniques make it impossible to choose any single species as typical of the stingless bees – the honey makers who mark the mid-point between the loose organization of the bumblebee and the complex community of the hive.

We do not know a great deal about stingless bees although scientists have studied them for years – particularly those that live in South America. Perhaps when you grow up you may become an entomologist and discover how the queens mate, what causes these bees to swarm, and why the queen-mother tolerates her royal daughters, while Her Majesty, the honeybee queen, does not.

However, we have learned that a community of stingless bees, like that of all social species, consists of an egg-laying queen, workers and, at certain seasons, drones; that a colony's population varies from a few hundred to thousands; and that they care for their young as solitary bees do – workers fill the brood-cells with bee-bread, the queen lays an egg upon it, the cells are then sealed and the babies develop without parental care.

No honey varies in value as much as that of stingless bees; often delicious, it is frequently nauseating. If not odorless, it has either a pleasant or disagreeable smell, while its color ranges from an attractive amber to an unappetizing blackish-brown. In some cases, it turns sour in a few hours; in others it can be stored indefinitely. But unlike the honeybee's golden treasure, it never granulates, always retaining its liquid form.

Despite the fact that the stingless bees' honey is apt to be of inferior quality, Australian and African tribesmen use it for sweetening, while the Indians of South and Central America prefer it to that produced by the "stinging flies" brought to the New World by white men. They also consider it excellent medicine and claim it cures many diseases. The honey is usually secured by "robbing" jungle-dwelling colonies because the nest-building habits of most species of stingless bees make it impossible to keep them in easily opened man-made hives.

THE HONEYBEE

If you place a honeybee under a microscope, each of the three ring-like segments that make up its body – the head, thorax and abdomen – are easily distinguished. Each of these sections has definite functions. The head carries the eyes, antennae, brain and mouth parts; the thorax supports the wings and legs; the abdomen, the digestive and reproductive organs and the heart. Here, too, are found the sting and wax-glands of the worker.

Bee Senses

EYES

Focusing the lens on each side of the flat, heart-shaped head, you'll see a large, compound eye – so called because it is made up of many tiny eyes set together – and three small, simple eyes arranged in a triangle in the middle of the forehead. This arrangement would be ideal for a traffic policeman, for it enables honeybees (who sleep with their eyes open) to see above, below, sideways, front and back at the same time!

Honeybees have excellent eyesight. This ability is developed by playflights – short excursions made by young bees in warm weather, during which they learn to recognize certain landmarks which they later use to chart their course when working in the fields. While the color sense of the honey makers is far more limited than that of the average human, they can perceive the ultra violet in sunshine – something man cannot do. Although they are able to distinguish black from white and recognize blue, purple and orange, they are partially color-blind, for red appears

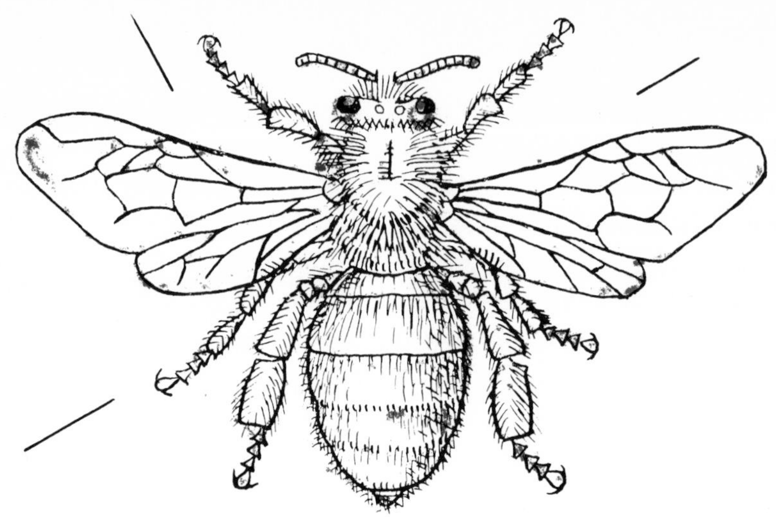

Photograph by U.S.D.A.

Honeybees have excellent eyesight because their two sets of eyes enable them to look above, below, sideways, front and back at the same time.

to them as gray. This explains the rareness of all-red flowers, which, overlooked by bees, must depend upon the fickle attentions of hummingbirds and butterflies for pollination.

The "oculist" who discovered that bees "know their colors," but are blind to red, was Karl von Frisch, who conducted a series of complicated experiments in the Botanical Gardens of Munich, Germany, in the 1930's. Placing a watch-crystal full of honey on a square of blue cardboard, he allowed foraging honeybees to eat their fill for several days. Then the scientist removed the original material and on either side of the exact spot where the blue square had been, he laid a red and blue one. Anxiously he awaited the insects' reaction – but, without a moment's hesitation, they alighted on the blue cardboard – proving they could recognize and remember color. Von Frisch did the same experiment thousands of times, using different colored squares, proving that, while honeybees had trouble recognizing some hues, they could distinguish many shades.

"NOSE"

Most insects employ their antennae merely as feelers, but bees use theirs as smellers as well, although other scent organs are scattered through the body. Rising out of the face, the antennae are among the most important "machines" in the flying chemical factory that is the honeybee. Under a lens, the two sections of the twin antennae are plainly seen, consisting of a straight segment at the base and a curving end portion made up of several segments – a worker has twelve of these, but uses only eight to distinguish the odors that seep to the sense plates through the thin places in the horn-like skin that covers them. The number of sense plates varies . . . the stay-at-home queen has the least, workers who use their antennae to find nectar have about six thousand, while drones have five times as many as their hard-working sisters.

Photograph courtesy Ontario Agricultural College

Worker honeybee cleaning her twin antennae after a foraging flight.

Although bees are unable to detect the aroma of distant objects, they are very keen-scented and their ability to recognize various odors is equal to that of man. Most of our knowledge of their sense of smell is due to Von Frisch's investigations. He filled a small dish with honey, to which he added a drop of perfume, then he set the dish in a cardboard box surrounded by several empty boxes of the same size. When his bees had learned the location of the first box, he shifted it, but they were not confused by the change and went directly to the aromatic honey. Next, a perfumed box containing no honey was substituted for the original container and the bees entered it without hesitation – proving that they were guided by a sense of smell. A careful experimenter, Von Frisch checked his findings, repeating the process many times, using dozens of different essences in his boxes. But there was no doubt – bees have the ability to recognize and remember scent.

This highly developed sense of smell plays a most important part in the life of the honeybee – for while it can distinguish flowers by color, its antenna enables it to sniff each species' distinctive bouquet. This is why a bee gathers nectar from only one kind of blossom during a foraging flight. The "nose" of a bee is also a valuable defensive weapon. Each colony has its own particular scent. The guards at a hive's entrance do not have to demand, "Friend or foe?" when a strange bee attempts to slip in and steal honey. Their antennae pick up the subtle difference in odor and they deal roughly with the intruder.

In addition to the scent shared in common by a colony, the queen has a personal fragrance. As long as the rest of her family can smell it, they are content; but if Her Majesty is removed, the insects become upset. Their sense of smell will not allow them to accept a strange queen – for she will, in addition to having her own odor, carry the scent of the hive from which she came. Like loyal peasants uprising against a foreign tyrant, the workers rebel against the usurper, sting her to death and throw her body out of the hive. However, if the queen is put in a small cage where the workers cannot reach her, she gradually acquires the new hive scent and, when released, is granted the honors due her rank.

MOUTH

The shape and structure of the mouth-parts of insects varies in accordance with their needs. The mouth of the moth and butterfly is designed for siphoning, the grasshopper's for chewing, the fly's for sponging, and that of the honeybee for sucking.

Few parts of a bee's anatomy are more complicated than its mouth, with its highly developed taste organs. It is located at the lower end of the face, between two heavy jaws which are hinged on the side and bite inwards. A worker's jaws are rounded at the end, while the larger ones of queens and drones have sharp points. The long tongue has a spoon-like end surrounded by delicate parts that fit together so that the insect can suck liquid through it, just as you drink soda through a straw.

If bees were human, they would probably drop six or seven lumps of sugar in their tea or coffee, for the sweeter the drink, the more they enjoy it. They recognize various degrees of sweetness and, when the fields are in full bloom, only visit those flowers whose nectar is richest in sugar. In the fall, unable to pick

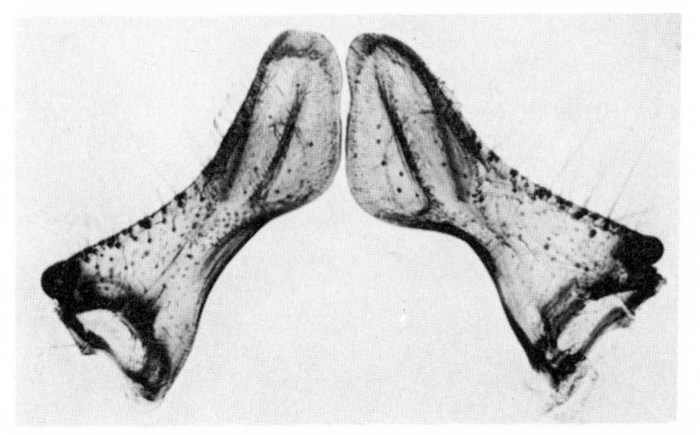

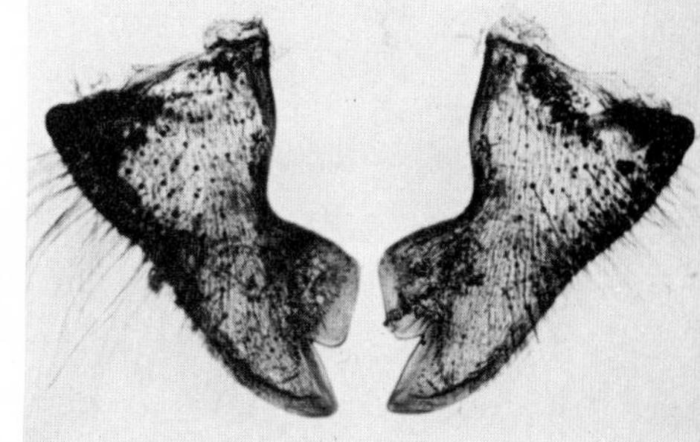

Photographs courtesy Ontario Agricultural College

A lens is needed to see the rounded jaws of a worker (left) or the sharp-pointed ones of queens and drones (right).

and choose, they are not so particular. Their taste sense is so keen that they can detect the most minute particle of salt in water — man would have to test the liquid chemically to discover it.

The hearing of bees is as dull as their taste is sharp. Although they live in a world of noise, they cannot tell one sound from another or distinguish pitch or tone. However, they are sensitive to vibrations. Oldtime beekeepers believed that the honeymakers could talk to each other and were convinced that, when a group of bees decided to leave their hive and set up a new home, their loud buzzing was a heated discussion of the best place to settle. In order to prevent the swarm from hearing what was being "said," it was the custom to bang tin pans together. While it is true that bees make a great deal of noise when swarming, they are not talking — for modern research has disclosed that all the sounds made by a bee are caused by their wings vibrating at various rates of speed. However, some people still think that making a noise causes a swarm to settle — but the truth is, they will do so anyway. The knocking together of pans was probably derived from an ancient English decree that ordered a beekeeper to ring a bell whenever his bees swarmed, in order to notify his neighbors that he was their owner. When a bell was not available, tin pans served to make enough noise to give the required alarm.

"And Away We Go!"

BY WING

No aircraft invented or steered by man flies as well as a honeybee. Capable of carrying weights heavier than themselves, they soar and hover in the air, zoom upward, dive downward, their "propellers" beating the air 11,400 times a minute. Bees are biplanes – that is, they have two sets of wings on each side of the thorax: two large front ones and a smaller pair in the rear. Loosely speaking, the four wings can be considered as two, for they are joined by tiny hooks and work together, making a figure-of-eight – up, forward, down, and back – the movement being governed by various muscles. When loaded with a full cargo, a bee cruises at about fifteen miles an hour. While flights five miles long have been recorded, they normally range about a mile and a half.

BY FOOT

Can you comb and brush your hair with your feet, walk up a smooth wall or across a ceiling?

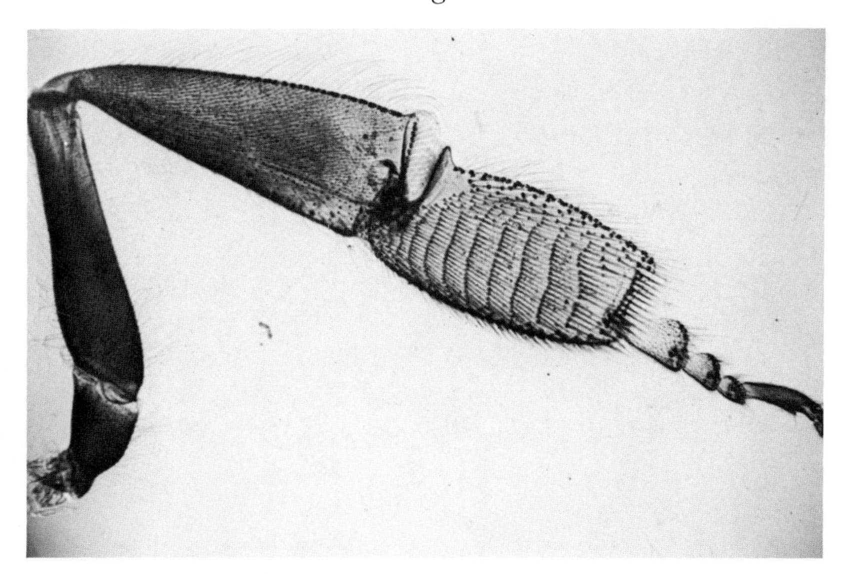

Photograph courtesy Ontario Agricultural College

Bees' legs, like those of humans, are divided into three sections, but the insects have claws instead of toes.

Impossible? Not for a bee. It does all these things and many more with its six legs which, like ours, are divided into three parts: a *femur* or thigh; a *tibia,* or shank; and a *tarsus,* or foot. Instead of toes, their feet end in sharp claws which have a sticky pad between them. These claws provide a means of clinging to rough objects, while the pads enable them to walk over smooth surfaces such as glass.

Unlike humans who move a leg at a time, bees step forward with three at once: the front and rear legs on one side and the middle leg on the opposite side. The front legs have antennae-cleaners – sort of built-in dust rags through which the insects run their feelers when dirty, just as a hunter pushes a cloth through the barrel of a used gun. All six legs are covered with a thick coat of hair which catches and holds pollen. However, although a strong colony will consume close to forty pounds of pollen in a season, a far greater amount of the golden dust never reaches the hive – it is transferred from one flower to another as the worker forages. Because bees are the only insects that raise

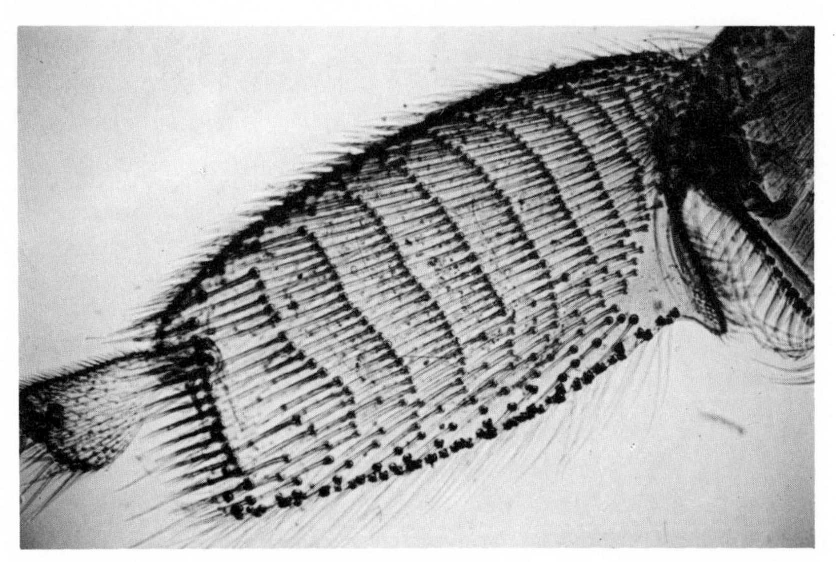

Photograph courtesy Ontario Agricultural College

Close-up view of pollen brush on the leg of a worker bee.

their young on pollen, workers have special tools to gather the tremendous quantities they need – a growth of thick hair that forms "pollen brushes" on the first two sets of legs and a "pollen comb" on the hind legs. In addition, they have a "pollen basket," located on the rear legs, consisting of a slightly hollowed-out area surrounded by long, curved bristles.

Alighting on a flower, a worker gathers pollen grains with tongue and jaw, dampening them with honey and saliva so that they stick together. The moist mass is removed by the forelegs and swept up by the brushes on the middle legs – then, just as you clean a hairbrush by running a comb through it, the middle legs are thrust through the combs on each opposite hind leg – scraping off the pollen and forcing it into the basket. Any moist pollen caught outside the brushes is picked up by the middle legs, which are also used to pat and press down the bulging baskets. When they are full, the bee flies homeward, enters the hive, examines the various cells and finally chooses one that suits her. Clutching the end of the cell with her forelegs, the hind ones crossed inside, the worker removes the pollen pellets with a scissor-like motion. Usually a younger member of the family takes over the chore of breaking up the pollen pellets and packing them properly, while the forager, her cargo discharged, zooms back to the fields, seeking another load.

Sting

Everyone knows two facts about *Apis mellifera:* it makes honey and can inflict a powerful sting.

Yet bees are among the most good-natured of insects and they use the sharp-pointed lance attached to the tip of the abdomen as a weapon only when provoked. That is why experienced beekeepers, working without veil or gloves, can remove honey from a hive and rarely receive a single sting. Of course, it is difficult to believe this when one examines a swollen lip, ear, or cheek or in those tense moments when a shrill buzzing bee circles your head, goes into a power dive and then burrows itself in your hair. Nor is it any consolation to know that, when a bee stings, it dies – all the victim realizes is that he is most uncomfortable.

There is good reason for this. A bee's sting is as sharp as a surgeon's scalpel, as tough as tungsten steel and finely barbed at the end, like a fishhook. This means that it can be driven in easily enough, but the barbs make pulling it out of flesh difficult. At the base, inside the body, is the poison-sac which forces venom into the hollow sting. This is what causes the pain – the prick of the barb is no worse than that of a needle. Bees often sting each other to death – the first to jab being the victor. Incidentally, it is only the hard-working females who sting men or animals, drones have no sting at all, while the curved one of the queen can be used over and over again, but only on other queens.

The Bee Family

WORKERS

How many bees would you guess live in a hive – a hundred, five hundred, or a thousand?

No matter which figure you choose, it is far too low, for a single colony normally consists of 35,000 to 60,000 inhabitants! In every hive there is always one queen, a few drones – except during the winter months – and thousands of workers. While

Photograph courtesy Ontario Agricultural College

Meet the three members of the honeybee family – queen, worker and drone.

every resident of the community resembles the others, just as members of the same family do, each group has certain physical characteristics that make performing their special duties possible.

Perhaps, because of her rank, we should begin with the queen. But the simple truth is – Her Majesty is no ruler, for, in the hive, no member of the colony competes with another, all have the same interests and share and share alike, and none can live independently of the others. So first place must go to the workers, who perform almost every chore necessary to maintain the hive.

Workers are really undeveloped females, who, among other things produce honey, gather and pack pollen, make wax, care for the young, clean house, act as guards, build comb and "air condition" the hive by standing in rows near the entrance, beating their wings, thus creating a cooling draft. However, workers cannot lay fertile eggs. They literally work themselves to death – living but six weeks. Their adult life is divided into three periods. They spend ten days tending the young, depending upon their

Photograph courtesy Ontario Agricultural College

When ladened with pollen a worker looks like a cowboy wearing yellow chaps.

senses of touch and smell to carry out their duties in the dark of the hive. Another ten days is devoted to housekeeping, construction and acting as guards. During this time, workers take short flights, to familiarize themselves with the neighborhood. Because of their duties, young workers are called "house" or "nurse" bees – when they are three weeks old and begin to collect pollen and nectar, they become "field" bees.

You probably have seen field bees sipping nectar which they store in their honey stomach, or crop, where it is changed into honey by chemical action during the homeward flight. This stomach has nothing to do with digestion, it merely holds the nectar while it is acted upon by body secretions. Incidentally, one worker could never make a pound of honey – she would have to visit a quarter of a million flowers in a day and fly a distance equal to two complete trips around the world to gather enough nectar!

Once inside the hive, a field bee transfers the contents of her crop to a younger worker, who mixes it thoroughly by forcing it

Photograph courtesy Ontario Agricultural College

Nurse bees carefully inspecting the brood comb that contains their unborn sisters.

in and out of her honey stomach and rolling it about on her tongue; adding more chemicals and removing much of the moisture. The house bee then carries the liquid to a cell. Her wings unhook where fastened together, slide on top of each other, and she crawls inside. Using her tongue as a brush, she lines the cell walls with honey or adds to the store already there. The excess water in the honey is slowly evaporated by the "air conditioners" and when ripe is capped with wax and keeps indefinitely.

Honeybees mold wax into food storage vaults and cradles. Nothing men and machines do with building materials to make architects' dreams come true is as fabulous as the wax-city of the bee. The accurate angles of their six-sided cells amaze mathematicians; they astonish engineers with their strength and capacity; and they are admired by entomologists as perfect insect nurseries. Nor is there a more artistic object in all of Nature than a honeycomb – two single sheets of six-sided horizontal cells, arranged back to back, the open ends facing in opposite directions.

Photograph courtesy Ontario Agricultural College

Just emerged worker crawls over capped cells and empty nurseries.

Photograph by Ewing Galloway

Insect engineers on the job — two workers constructing comb with beeswax.

Photograph courtesy A. I. Root Co.
It is not difficult to assemble section-boxes and insert foundation.

While human construction crews depend upon factories to furnish building materials, bees make their own. Whenever comb is needed, a group of workers gorge themselves on honey (it takes about six pounds to make one pound of wax) and form a living curtain inside the hive, each bee reaching up with her front legs to grasp the hind legs of the one above. Their closely packed bodies raise the hive temperature to about 97° F. – and in a short while a fluid appears on the lower side of the abdomen. This liquid is wax and, as it oozes out, it hardens into thin, transparent scales similar to those of fish. Using her rear legs to pry up the wax, the worker passes it to the front legs and on to the mouth then chews it into a soft, pliable mass. Now the wax is ready to be used to repair old and build new comb.

In order to save honeybees time and effort and start them building even and parallel comb, beekeepers provide them with "comb foundation" – a sheet of pure beeswax, stamped out to form the base of an artificial honeycomb. It is exactly like the natural product in every respect, except that its walls are heavier, a feature that enables the insects to use the excess wax to draw out the cells. Even a narrow strip of foundation will start them building perfectly shaped comb, but a full sheet insures that only worker cells will be molded, thus increasing the amount of honey that will be gathered. Without foundation, bees fashion two sizes of cells – the larger holds the eggs that hatch out drones (who gather no honey) while the smaller ones are for the eggs that develop into workers.

Besides manufacturing honey and wax, workers also make bee-bread from pollen and saliva, for use as baby food. Often they are flying bottles of glue, for they collect gummy secretions of certain plant and tree leaf-buds, to cement rough places in the hive, fill in cracks, or spread as varnish over honeycomb – using their tongues as trowel and brush. The name of this sticky substance is propolis, stemming from the Greek *pro* (before) and *polis* (city), because of the bees' habit of partially closing up the entrance of their wax city with it – instinct prompting them to block out snow, rain, cold and unwanted visitors.

It is no easy task for a house bee to remove propolis from the pollen baskets of a field bee. Using her jaws, she pulls with all her might, while her sister strains in the opposite direction. This tug of war continues until all the "bee-glue" is gathered. Then it is used immediately. Although propolis has some value as a treatment for burns, it is a nuisance to the beekeeper, gluing the hive-frames together and staining the comb. However, despite the fact that the sturdy construction of modern hives should make the insect's use of propolis unnecessary, the chances are that bees "know" pretty well what they are doing when they seal cracks and contract the doorway to their home.

DRONES

Although workers think nothing of toiling all day and often labor far into the night, "air conditioning" the hive, male bees do nothing but eat and sleep. Because of the deep buzzing noise they make as they fly, they are called drones, a word often applied to persons who are not willing to do their share of work. The drones' angry buzz gives the impression that they are ferocious, but these lazy creatures never attack anyone, for they have no sting.

A drone not only differs from his sisters in his attitude toward toil, but also in the shape of his body. Larger than that of a worker, it is broad and blunt. Since he never goes foraging, his tongue is short, there are no baskets on his hind legs, nor does he have any wax secreting glands. Without tools to add to the colony's food supply and lacking any defensive weapon, drones would seem to have very little value to a hive. But the workers feed and care for them because they know that the swiftest of their brothers will mate with the queen in mid-air — overtaking her with his large and powerful wings. Then he dies.

All during the spring and summer months, drones are tolerated, but with the approach of fall, when nectar is scarce, they are pushed out of the hive to die — for with the mating season

Photograph courtesy Ontario Agricultural College

Although larger than their hard-working sisters, drones never help them.

over, they are of no use. Moreover, every sip of honey they drink drains the precious hoard that will carry the colony through the winter.

The most remarkable thing about a drone is that he has no father, for, unlike the eggs of an unmated hen, which never hatch, those of a queen bee who has never met a male develop into drones. On her return from a mating flight, a queen bee can lay either fertile or unfertile eggs at will — the former become workers and queens, the latter, drones.

QUEEN

The queen is the largest bee in the colony, with a long, slender, graceful body. Because she is not expected to work, she has no "tools." But unlike a drone, Her Majesty does not lead a carefree life. In fact, no human sovereign works as hard, for, being the only fully developed female in the hive, her task is to become the mother of all the other members of the community. But she

Photograph courtesy Ontario Agricultural College

The long, pointed body of Her Majesty, the queen, extends far beyond the tips of her folded wings giving her a graceful form.

never shows the slightest interest in her children. It is the workers who feed, care for and defend the babies. A queen is nothing but an animated egg-laying machine that produces 1,500 eggs a day at intervals of thirty seconds, for a period of three to five years. The egg-laying season begins in February, rises to a peak in midsummer and stops in late fall, when the supply of nectar drops.

Egg-laying

Before laying a single egg, the queen examines the comb, to make sure that the workers who act as cleaners have done a thorough job. As she carries out her inspection, Her Royal Highness is surrounded by her "court" — bees who constantly offer her food and stroke her abdomen. When satisfied that the cells are spotless, she chooses one in the center and deposits a tiny gray, comma-

Photograph courtesy Ontario Agricultural College

A royal "coffee-break" — a member of the court feeds the queen-mother.

shaped egg within its walls. Then, moving slowly to another cell, she repeats the process. In early spring, only worker eggs are laid – insuring that, when flowers are in blossom, there will be enough

Photograph courtesy Ontario Agricultural College

No, this isn't a balloon, it's the egg of a honeybee.

foragers to replenish the hive's stores. But in midsummer, both worker and drone eggs are placed in the comb.

After depositing several eggs, the queen rests briefly, takes some food from her attendants then goes back to work, placing the eggs in spirals until the entire comb, with the exception of the cells around the edges, is full. These outer cells contain honey and bee-bread. The eggs hatch out in the order in which they were laid – those in the center first, those on the outside of the circle, last. Some never hatch and another egg is placed beside each of them – for bees waste neither time nor space. As soon as the babies leave their cells, their mother returns and refills the empty nurseries.

Baby Grows Up

LARVA

When just laid, an egg lies horizontally, but it gradually rises to a perpendicular position on the bottom of the cell. It hatches in three days, releasing a grub called a larva (plural, larvae). Nothing is more helpless – it is blind, has no antennae, eyes or legs – and it could not live were it not for the constant attention of the nurse bees and the protection of the cell walls. The one thing that a larva has is a stomach, and its appetite is so great that it consumes 1,300 meals a day!

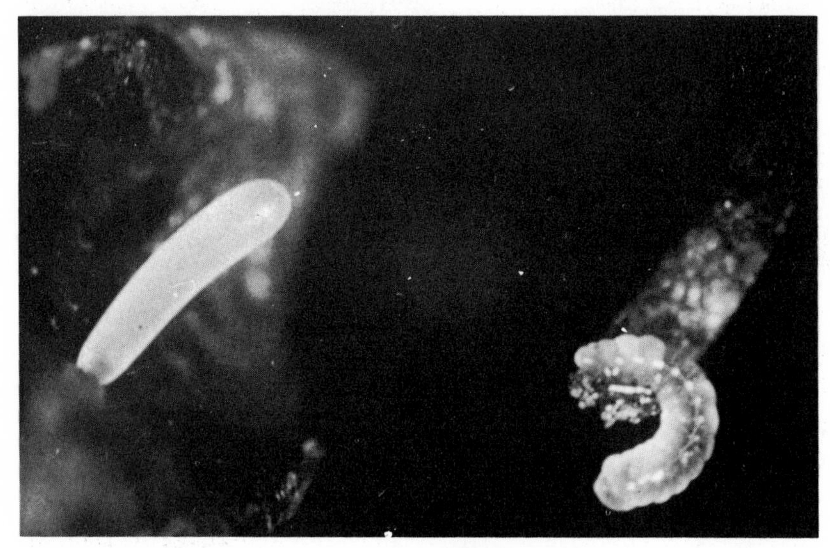

Photograph courtesy Ontario Agricultural College

A newly emerged larva (right) looks just like a legless caterpillar.

Like human infants, the more larvae eat, the faster they grow. In three days, they are 240 times their original size, but the hard covering that encases the body does not expand – it stretches like an elastic band and gets tighter and tighter. In time, it becomes rigid and the larvae stop eating, while a new body case is formed under the old one. When it is complete, the baby wiggles like a snake and the motion causes the outer layer to split and fall off – but soon the new case too becomes stiff and has to be cast aside. This process is called moulting and bee larvae go through it five times in all.

From the third day on, most larvae are fed honey and pollen by their nurses, but a few continue to receive the creamy-white food which has been served to them since birth for an additional two days. This mysterious substance, called royal jelly, is formed in the throat glands of young workers. It is so rich in vitamins that some doctors, anxious to furnish a supply to their patients, have paid $500 a pound for it. But royal jelly – and no food has a more appropriate name – has a far greater value than this. *For*

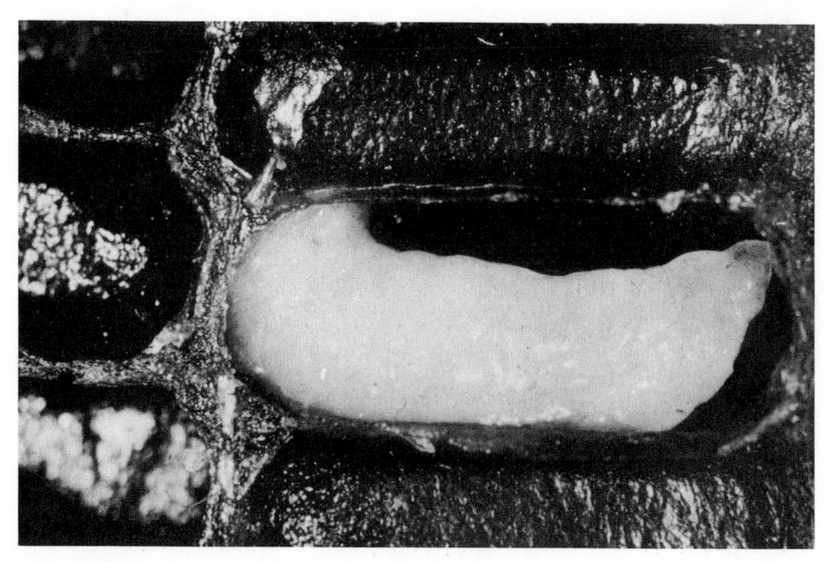

Photograph courtesy Ontario Agricultural College

This is how a worker larva looks in its cell just before pupation.

any worker grub that eats nothing else for the first five days of its life will develop into a queen! However, powerful as the magic of royal jelly is, it cannot change a drone into a queen.

The cells containing princesses are enlarged by combining them with the adjoining ones – for an ordinary cell is too small to hold a queen's large body. When finished, the royal chamber is peanut-shaped and takes up as much room as three ordinary cells.

Constantly receiving either coarse food or royal jelly, larvae grow so quickly that when only five days old they are 1,570 times bigger than at birth! As they eat, they frequently shift position, but when mature, they turn their heads toward the cell opening and remain motionless. Workers then seal the nurseries with wax. But this capping, unlike that placed over honey, is not pure. It is porous and consists of often re-used wax, bits of cocoon and other debris. Queen-cells get special attention, the capping being drawn out to a tapering point and indented, like the sides of a thimble.

PUPA

Once the brood is sealed, the larvae spin a cocoon around their bodies, moving back and forth in the cell many times before completing their "mummy case." The baby is now a "pupa." It lies on its back while changes take place within its body. The silk glands in the mouth vanish, the three divisions of the adult insect appear, and the eyes, legs and wings take shape. When mature, the young bee wiggles out of its silk covering, bites through the cap on its cell and joins its grown-up brothers and sisters. These four stages in a bee's development – egg, larva, pupa and adult – are called metamorphosis (Greek, "to change shape"). A queen reaches adulthood faster than other bees – probably because of the extra amount of royal jelly she receives, while workers take less time than drones.

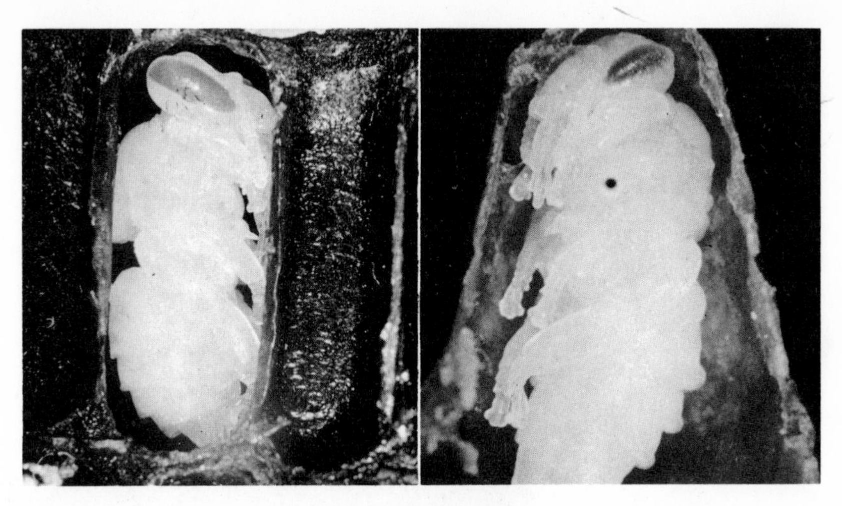

Photographs courtesy Ontario Agricultural College

Can you tell by looking at the shape of these two cells which one of these nearly mature pupae is a worker and which one is a queen?

Once out of the cell, the young bee crawls about the hive. No attention is paid to the newcomer. After one day of freedom, workers start feeding the older larvae and when they are six days old, they serve royal jelly. Usually, every bee of the same age does the same task – the continual hatching of eggs providing a constant number of workers to carry out the various activities of the hive.

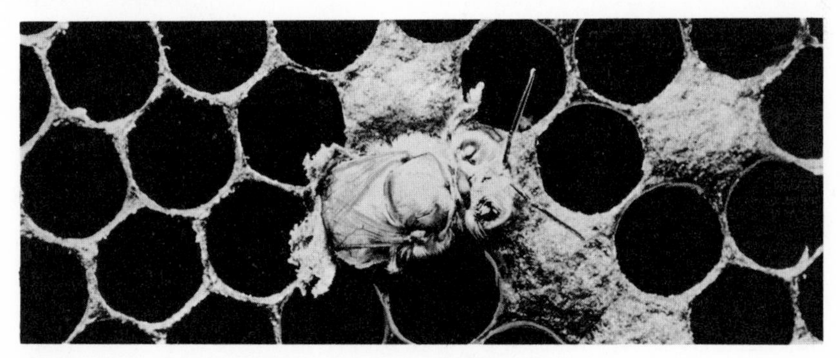

Photograph courtesy Ontario Agricultural College

Free at last – a young bee clambers out of its cell.

Photograph courtesy American Museum of Natural History

Brood comb showing different stages in the life history of the honeybee.

Royal Rivals

No such simple routine is followed by a young queen. Her only concern is to destroy her sisters of royal rank. With sting and jaw, she upholds the fundamental law of the hive – only one queen to a colony.

Before she emerges from her cell, a queen utters her battle-cry – a high, piping note – warning other would-be rulers that she is ready to fight for her domain. If answered, Her Majesty rushes into battle. The two queens try to seize each other in their jaws and, once they get a firm grip, attempt to sink their curved swords into their opponent's armor. Death ends the struggle and the loser's body is thrown out of the hive by the workers, just as they remove any unclean object.

If no other queens have matured, the young ruler crawls over the comb, seeking cells that contain her royal sisters. Sometimes the workers help her tear them down, at other times, she rips them apart without aid. If they hold nearly developed adults, the queen stings them over and over again – if they shelter grubs, the defenceless creatures are picked out, piece by piece.

Her rivals disposed of, the queen is now ready for her mating flight. Then she will begin the task of laying thousands of eggs – working as long hours as any of her subjects – receiving no reward save the constant attention workers pay to the queen-

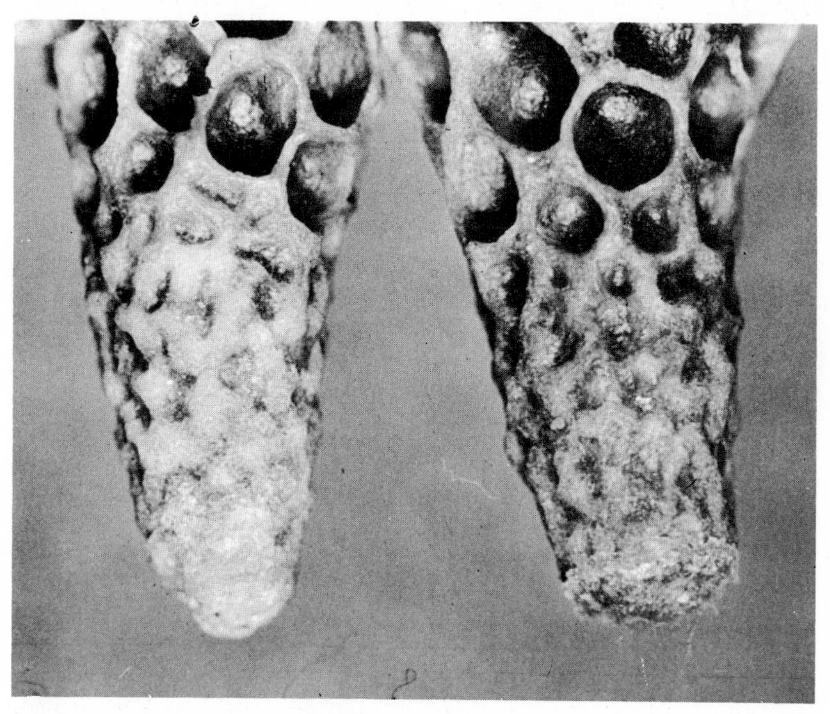

Photograph courtesy Ontario Agricultural College

Queen cells – one on right just ready to hatch as bees have removed wax covering from tip of cell.

Photograph by U.S.D.A.

Close-up of a brood frame showing large area of sealed brood.

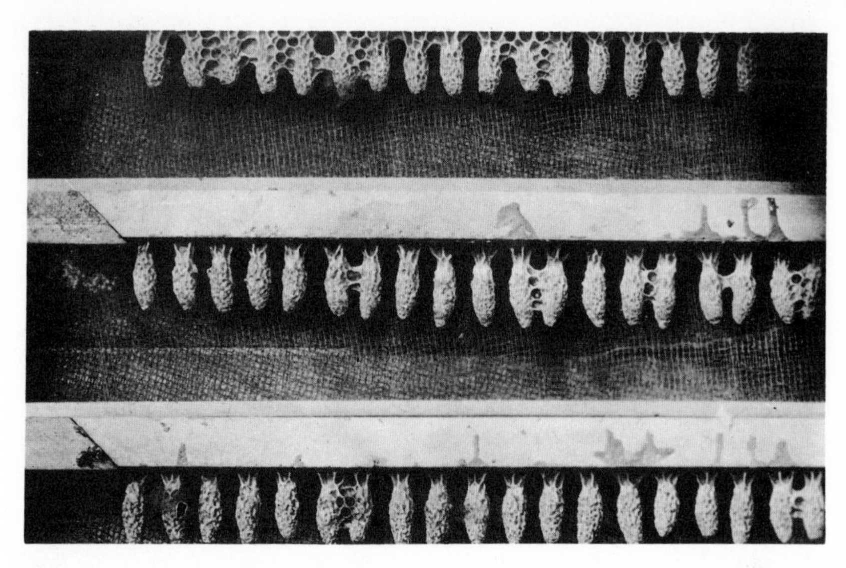

Photograph courtesy A. I. Root Co.

A job for the specialist – raising queens to sell to beekeepers.

mother of their colony. Her peaceful reign comes to a close when peanut-shaped cradles appear in the brood comb – then Her Royal Highness, accompanied by thousands of her court, leaves the hive to found a new city of wax.

The Swarm

The old queen's departure from the colony is one of the most fascinating migrations in the world. There is nothing rash in bees leaving the security of the hive and their hard-earned food supply, nor is their flight into the unknown an impulsive action. It is undertaken in order to make sure that the insects will set up new colonies and perpetuate themselves. This mass movement of bees who leave their old quarters to set up housekeeping elsewhere is called swarming. It takes place in mid-June or early July, when the hive is filled with newly hatched workers and the comb is crammed with honey, pollen and larvae.

The royal proclamation, announcing that the time has come to leave the hive, is the laying of queen eggs. The bustling activity of the field bees gives way to a "sit-down-strike," as they stay at home, instead of gathering food, gorge themselves with honey and hang in great clusters from the comb. Meanwhile, with thousands of babies emerging from the cells, the queen-mother no longer attempts to fill the empty nurseries and her attendants do not offer her food constantly. As a result, her abdomen shrinks, causing her body to become lighter – if it didn't, her wings, unused for months, would be unable to carry her to her new home.

Photograph by Ewing Galloway

Cluster of bees that have swarmed and settled on a branch.

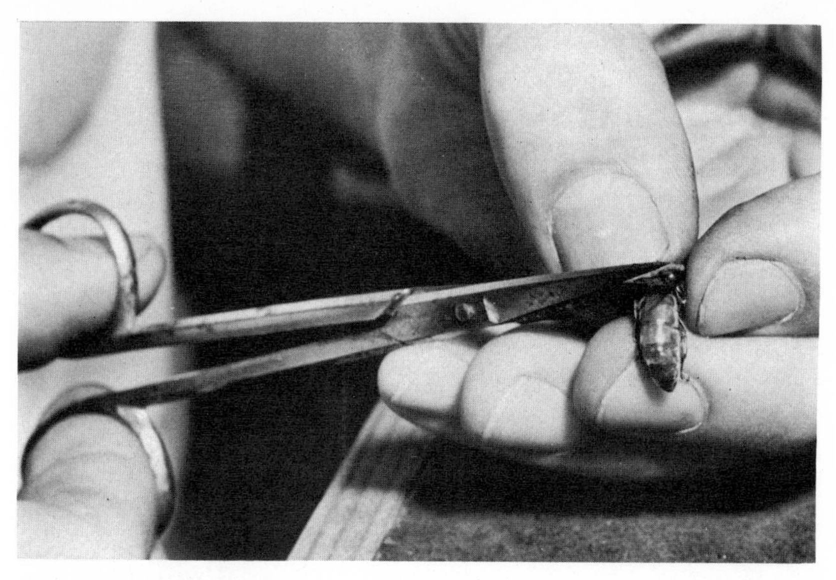

Photograph by U.S.D.A.

Clipping a queen's wings keeps her from flying out with a swarm.

When the first queen cell is capped (nine days after the egg is laid) and if the weather is pleasant, a strange silence falls over the hive. Suddenly, a stream of insects pours out, their wings creating the so-called musical "swarm-tone" as they circle about in the air, forming a dense cloud. After a few minutes of impetuous flight, they come to rest in a cluster. Usually they settle on a limb, stump, or fence, but often they land on lamp posts, ladders, walls or automobile bumpers. But no matter where the swarm alights, stragglers are guided to the spot by the scent given out by the quivering mass.

The queen does not lead the swarm, although she may be among the first to leave the old hive. Often she waits until at least half of the swarming bees have departed, but frequently she is the last to emerge. If she refuses to join the migration, her children fly aimlessly about and finally return home — making another attempt to swarm the next day. This time the queen joins them.

Photograph courtesy of Boston Herald

When swarming, bees are easily collected by beekeepers and carried to a hive.

Sometimes, instead of destroying her rivals, a young queen accompanies a second, or after-swarm. Occasionally, there may be additional after-swarms – but each contains a progressively smaller number of bees – all young workers best suited to carry out the chore of building a new wax city. At last the urge to swarm gives way to the age-old desire to preserve the routine of the hive and a young queen, thanks to her skill with sting and jaws, becomes the new queen-mother and the cycle begins once more.

While clustered, swarming bees are very good-natured – it is their one holiday and their tempers reflect it. A swarm is easily shaken into a container and then released into an empty hive, but the beekeeper must work quickly, for scout bees have been searching for a new home and, if they return and report before the swarm is hived, the bees soar away and it may be impossible to capture them.

The Hive

Swarming bees are perfectly content to set up housekeeping in hollow trees, nail kegs, empty boxes, or between the rafters of a building, but their comb cannot be inspected regularly, removed, or rearranged in such locations. This can be done only in a modern wooden hive containing movable and transferable frames.

EARLY HIVES

Lacking tools and imagination, early man copied the "bee trees" he found in the woods and made simple hives from sec-

Photograph by U.S.D.A.

Bees in the United States produce half the beeswax we use. Most of it comes from imperfect combs like the one seen on the left in this picture.

tions of hollow logs, covering the open tops and bottoms with slabs. As he became more civilized and learned to weave, straw was braided into "skeps" (Old English for basket) – perhaps you have seen pictures of these dome-shaped structures in a book of fairy tales. Skeps are still widely used in Europe where lumber is expensive, particularly in Holland where they are often made in the shape of St. Ambrose. Pottery hives were also common in former times – sometimes they were molded to resemble huge heads and the bees used the wide-open mouth for an entrance!

While these early hives provided an easily gathered honey harvest, they had one great fault – in order to remove the comb, most of the colony had to be destroyed. So as man developed tools and became skilled in their use, he attempted to build an enclosure that would not only shelter bees and provide them with ideal working conditions, but would also allow their owners to examine the hive and take out surplus honey without harming its makers. The problem's solution was a seemingly simple one – a hive containing movable frames on which the bees could fashion their comb and equipped with a detachable roof. This would allow for the addition of an upper story or "super" for honey storage, which when full, could be removed. Yet it took hundreds of years and thousands of experiments before such a hive was designed.

The first improvement was made by the ancient Greeks, who inserted wooden bars in their flower-pot shaped hives, but little more was accomplished until the invention of a glass-sided, single comb observation hive, in the seventeenth century. Now, for the first time, man could actually see what went on inside a hive.

Strangely enough, a blind man used the "glass hive" to the greatest advantage. This genius was François Huber, a Swiss naturalist, who lost his sight at the age of fifteen, but spent years studying the habits of the honeybee through the eyes of his devoted servant, François Burnens. Huber would suggest an experiment, outline a method of procedure and evaluate the results, while the faithful Burnens did the physical work. Once the latter individually caught every bee in two hives – a task that took eleven days – stopping only to rest his eyes when his blind employer insisted. By degrees, the trained scientist and his skilled but uneducated assistant learned more about bees than other men had in centuries. Using this knowledge, Huber designed the first movable comb hive. This was known as the "leaf hive" because the frames were hinged together at one end, opening like a book.

As the years passed, Huber's hive was modified by many different experimenters. Finally, on October 30, 1851, an American minister, Lorenzo Lorraine Langstroth, conceived the idea of a movable bar frame hive with a detachable roof. He installed trial models on a plot of land in West Philadelphia which is now part of the campus of the University of Pennsylvania. Langstroth soon discovered that he "had made no invention at all, but rather a perfect revolution in beekeeping." In 1852 he was granted a patent on his hive – and it is still considered the standard today. Yet, despite the fact that Longstroth made commercial beekeeping possible, he did not become rich. He died a poor man.

Still revered wherever man cares for bees, Langstroth received his greatest honor on October 20, 1951 – the centennial year of his great achievement. On that date, the Morris Arboretum of the University of Pennsylvania dedicated the Langstroth Bee Garden – a group of hives in an area planted with flowers and shrubs valuable to bees. Highlight of the program was the unveiling of a memorial bench inscribed with a summary of Langstroth's achievements.

MODERN HIVES

Each part of a standard hive is separable and interchangeable and fits into the others. Usually, to avoid contact with the damp ground, the hive rests on a stand – an arrangement that allows the erection of an alighting board or ramp that enables a

Photograph by U.S.D.A.

Braided straw hives or "skeps" are still used in many parts of Europe.

ladened bee to enter a hive easily. The hive itself consists of a floor or bottom board on which a topless and bottomless box called the brood chamber rests. This is where the queen lays eggs and the babies are reared. Inside this section is the most important furniture in the bee's apartment house — the removable frames that hold the comb. They are made of four pieces of wood fastened together. The top bar is slightly longer than the one on the bottom and rests on a ledge — a device that gives the frames very little contact with the hive-body and spaces them uniformly apart.

On top of the brood chamber, one or more supers are fitted. These are merely additional four-sided boxes containing frames on which the bees build comb. There are two types of frames: extracting and section-holders. Honey from extracting frames is cut out with a special knife or removed from the comb by cen-

Photograph courtesy A. I. Root Co.

Frames wired with foundation save bees many hours of work.

Photograph by U.S.D.A.

The whirling centrifugal motion of an extractor throws honey out of a comb. Then the comb is replaced in the hive for the bees to fill again.

trifugal force – just as cream is separated from milk in a diary. The comb is then put back in the hive for the bees to refill. Section-holders get their name from the thin, square, wooden boxes or sections in which comb honey is sold in stores. Beekeepers arrange these so that the insects will place about a pound of honey in each one. Extracted honey is cheaper than comb honey because it saves the wax, which is more valuable economically than the hive's golden treasure. Taking honey from the supers does no harm to the colony, if enough is left to provide for the needs of the bees.

The number of supers varies with the needs of the colony – the more honey it gathers, the greater the number that are added. Normally, in order to prevent the queen from laying eggs in a

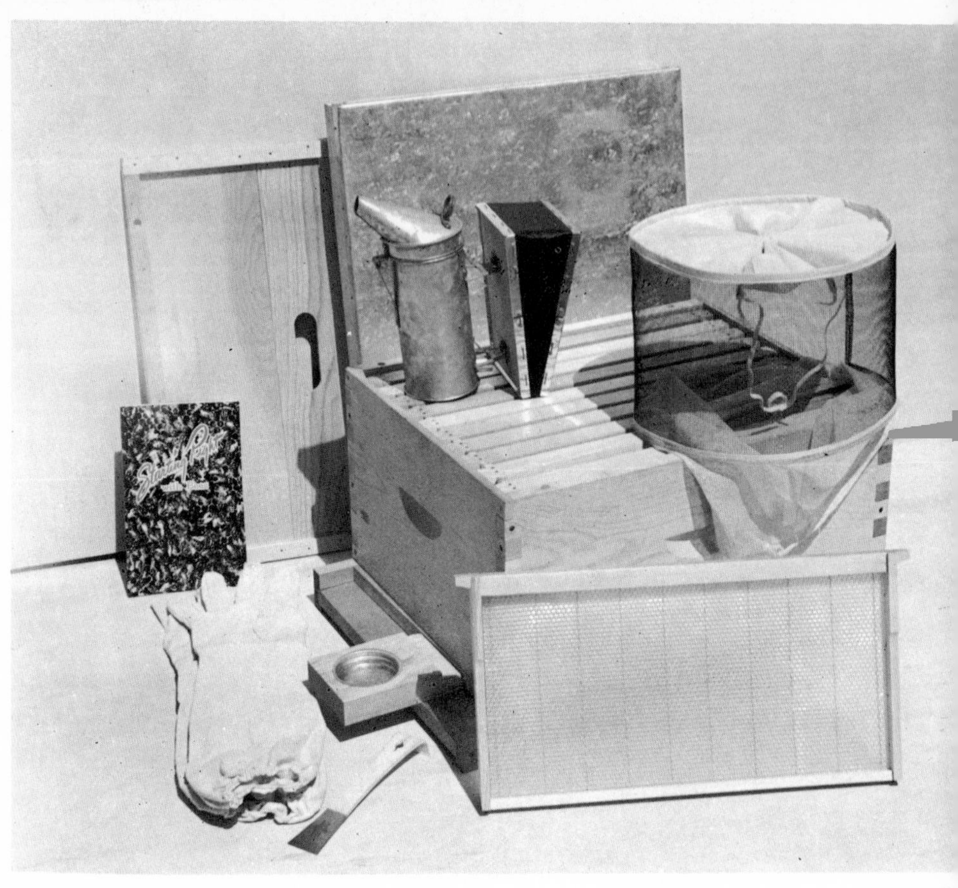

Photograph courtesy A. I. Root Co.

Beekeeping equipment: smoker and veil on top of hive body; gloves and hive-tool at right. Just behind foundation-wired frame a feeder is inserted into hive entrance.

super, a wire mesh is placed across the top of the brood chamber. Workers have no difficulty in crawling through the holes to reach frames in the supers, but they are too small for a queen. However, when more brood comb is wanted, she is allowed access to additional supers. All supers are capped by an inner lid and the entire hive is protected by a close-fitting outer cover that guards the bees and their handiwork from the weather.

Photograph by U.S.D.A.

Two or three puffs of smoke will quiet the residents of a hive.

Parts of a Modern Bee Hive

Cut Away to Show Interior

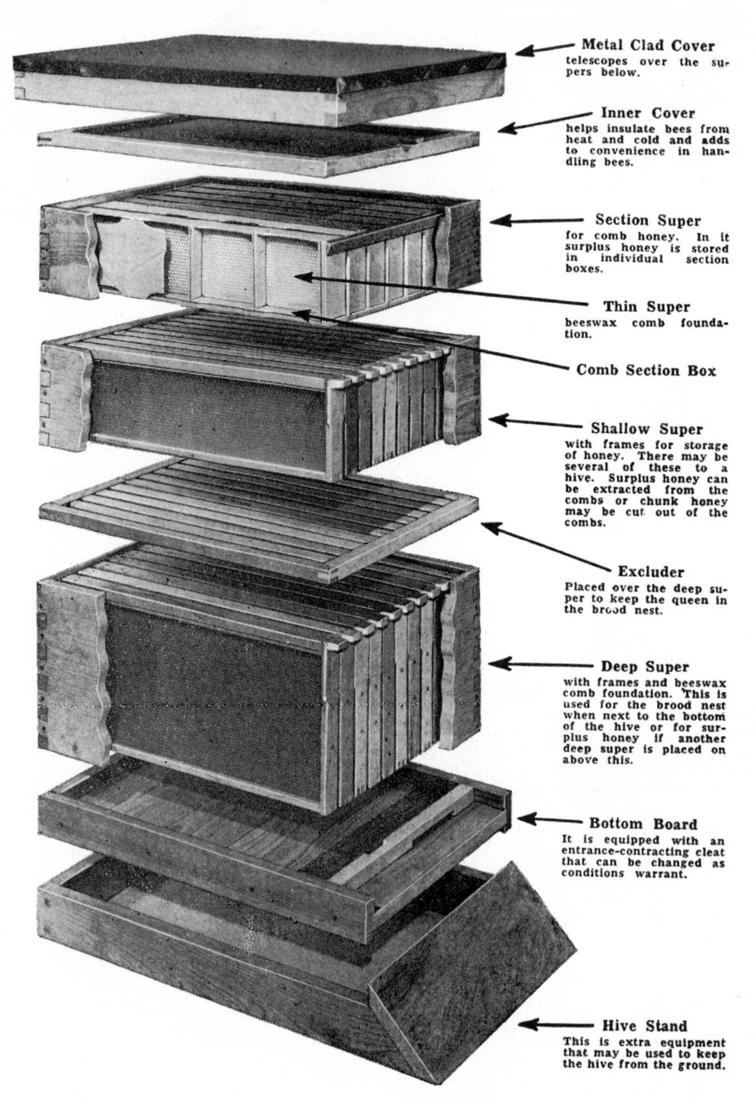

Photograph courtesy A. I. Root Co.

All parts of a modern hive are standard in size and interchangeable.

OPENING A HIVE

Would you like to gather honey from a hive? There isn't much danger of being stung if you avoid sudden motions and the weather is warm. While experienced beemen scorn the use of gloves, hat, veil and trousers tucked into high boots, it would be better if you wore them. Avoid dark clothes, for, as a general rule, when bees are in a stinging mood, they seem to be less irritated by light-colored clothing. Be sure and put a hive tool in your pocket. This efficient gadget is made of spring steel and has one flat and one hooked end. The flat edge is used to pry up the cover of the hive, to separate one super from another, or to force frames apart, while the hooked edge is ideal for scraping wax and propolis from the frames and bottom boards.

One other tool is needed to explore the mysteries of the hive – a smoker. This is nothing but a portable tin stove with an attached bellows and nozzle. When the bellows are squeezed, air is

Photograph by Ewing Galloway

One of these frames contains a queen cell. Can you find it?

forced through the rags, shavings, pine needles, or rotten wood used for fuel and drives a smoke cloud toward the bees. This quiets them and they lose all desire to sting, so working with them is a simple matter. It takes skill to use a smoker correctly, however. If the bellows are pumped too hard, the fuel bursts into flame; if not hard enough, the fire goes out. When either of these mishaps occur, a novice beekeeper is apt to discover his clothing is not as bee-proof as he thought!

Dressed properly, hive tool in pocket and smoker in hand, stand at one side of the hive and blow a light puff of smoke on the alighting board. Now insert the flat end of the hive tool under the outer cover and slowly remove it. The main thing is to avoid jarring the bees. Then lift the inner cover up a little and send a puff or two into the gap between it and the super. Almost immediately you will hear a difference in the humming of the bees and when it drops off to a steady low buzz, you may open the hive. Now the frames can be lifted out without danger of being stung, although an occasional whiff of smoke may be necessary to soothe the colony. Be careful not to pinch any bees – merely push them aside gently – and they will pay no attention to you while you gather a rich harvest.

Bee Behavior

DANCES

Humans rarely dance for joy when faced with an additional work-load, but bees always do. When a forager finds an abundant food supply, she announces the discovery by dancing. Honeybees execute two different dances – a round dance and a tail-wagging dance. The steps tell what flowers have been found,

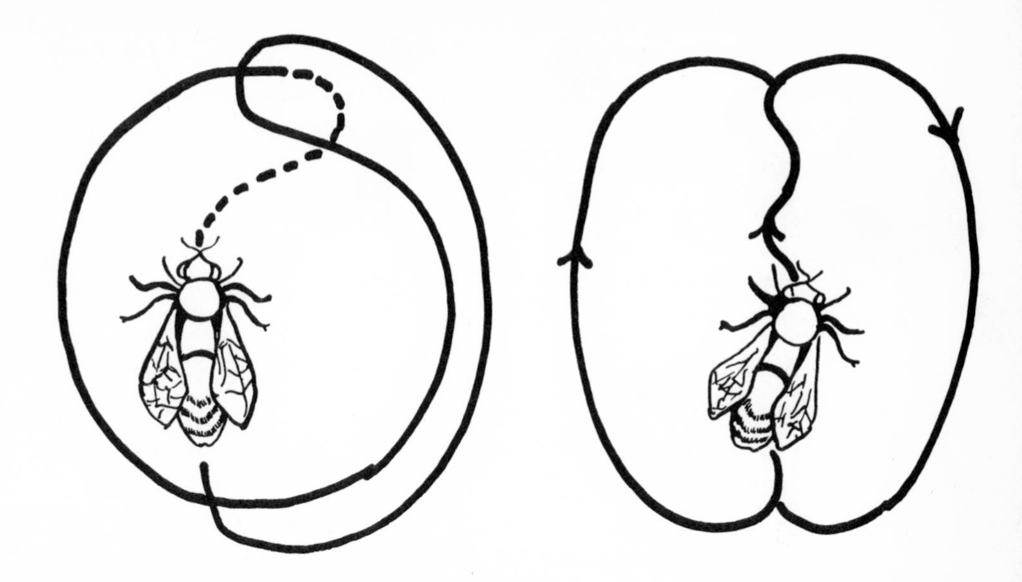

Bee dances – left, round dance performed when food is less than 100 yards from hive; right, figure-of-eight dance executed when it is farther away.

how rich their nectar and pollen, where located and how to reach them.

The round dance is the simpler of the two, for it does not inform the other bees in what direction to fly. It is only used when blossoms are less than one hundred yards away. First the dancer climbs up the comb, then, in a tight oval, whirls to the right and left. While she rotates, other workers touch her with their antennae, get the scent of the flowers she has found, then stream out of the hive, circle about until they see the blossoms, zoom down, pick up the hive odor left by the dancer and begin their labors.

If the food is over one hundred yards away, the dancer performs a figure-of-eight on the comb, wagging her abdomen from side to side. The number of wags informs the watchers the distance flown, while the direction of the dance indicates the location of the treasure. If the dancer goes up the comb, it means that it is in the direction of the sun; if down, away from it. A dance at an angle tells the bees to fly to the left or right. The only thing a tail-wagging dance does not reveal is how high the food is from the ground – there is no "step" signifying height.

ROBBING

When the supply of nectar is low, bees are apt to steal from another colony, rather than go foraging. Once they become thieves, they rarely reform and prefer to "get rich quick" at their neighbors' expense.

Robber bees never attempt to enter a well-populated hive, for they know it would be useless. They always choose weak colonies. A pilfering bee tries to slip by the guards at the entrance without being stung to death. If she succeeds, she moves slowly about, hoping to give the impression that she isn't a stranger as she heads toward the unsealed honey cells, for if a resident becomes suspicious, the thief may pay for "breaking and entering" with her life. When challenged, the robber usually tries to escape, but often bluffs her way out of danger by standing her ground.

If successful in securing a load of honey, the worker flies home and spreads the good news. Immediately, a group of her sisters takes off for the treasure trove. While the weaker colony attempts to defend itself, all resistance is overcome in a short time.

TELLING TIME

Bees can tell time. Without this ability, they would waste much time and strength, for some flowers yield nectar only at

Photograph by U.S.D.A.

A worker bee enters a blossom to gather nectar or pollen for her colony.

Photograph courtesy Ontario Agricultural College

Special containers are used to ship bees when they are ordered by mail.

certain hours. For years, scientists thought that the rotation of the earth controlled the clock-like regularity with which workers foraged, but in 1956 it was established that bees have "built-in" clocks.

First a group of bees were trained to drink sugared water placed near their hive at sunset, in Paris, France. When the habit was firmly established, the insects were fed, rushed to New York City by airplane and placed in a room exactly like the one in which they had lived overseas. If the bees left their new hive to feed at about the same time as the Paris sunset, it would mean that some inner time signal controlled their actions. If they waited until the sun went down in New York City, it would show that some external influence was at work. The question was settled when the insects emerged at the same time as in their original home, paying no attention to the fact that there was a five-hour difference in time between Paris and New York City and that the sun — which they could not see — had not moved as far across the sky as would be the case in Paris.

WEATHER MAKING

Like all insects, bees are cold-blooded, and their body heat is that of the surrounding air. They are happiest in the summer, when the long days are bright and sunny. During the winter months, if the temperature of their hive drops below 57° F., they make their own "weather" by forming huge clusters on the comb.

These festoons are constantly in motion — the insects in the center wiggle from side to side, wag their antennae, surge forward and backward and wave their wings. Like a man swinging his arms on a cold day, this muscular activity warms the cluster. The generated heat is prevented from escaping by the close-packed bodies of the bees on the outside fringes. The cluster expands or contracts according to the prevailing temperature and the colder it is, the more the bees move about. They continually shift positions. Those on the inside change with the "insulators" and rest while their comrades take over "tending the furnace." Bees get the energy they need to warm themselves and each other by slowly eating honey — the cluster moving over the comb as the storage cells are emptied.

Uses of Honey

As indicated, honey varies in color, consistency and taste, depending upon its source. But clear and thin as water, or thick and brown as molasses, with a strong tang or a delicate flavor, it is an excellent energy-producing food. Although sugar manufactured from corn, beets and cane has reduced honey's importance to mankind, it still is widely used for sweetening. Moreover, it can be absorbed directly into the blood stream and does not require digestion, making it an ideal food for infants. Doctors prescribe it for coughs and colds, in the treatment of various diseases and in cases of stomach disorder. Honey can also be used as a dressing for cuts and burns, as it has both a soothing and antiseptic effect.

Commercially, honey is used in cosmetics, as a substitute for sugar in candy-making and also to sweeten beverages, cakes, custards, ice cream, jams, jellies, medicines, pies and preserves. Cakes and cookies keep better when prepared with honey because it absorbs moisture from air – which is the reason why wholesale bakers who ship their wares long distances use most of the eighty million pounds produced yearly in the United States.

Uses of Wax

Although mineral wax (a by-product of petroleum) and various plant waxes have largely replaced beeswax in art and industry, millions of pounds are still used every year. Chemists compound it in shoe blacking, furniture polish, ink, lubricants, paints, varnishes and hundreds of other products. When a dentist "takes an impression," he uses beeswax; shoemakers' thread is coated with it; while beekeepers consume vast quantities in providing their bees with the foundation that saves them time and effort.

The finest candles are made of beeswax. Unlike those molded

Photograph courtesy A. I. Root Co.

Honey in the comb is the sweetest of Nature's gifts to man.

from mineral or vegetable material that give off a greasy odor when burning, they fill the air with pleasant perfume. Beeswax has a very high melting point and this characteristic, plus its great resistance to moisture, makes it an excellent insulation for electric wires.

Lessons from the Hive

Man owes much to bees – honey, wax and most of his crops – so it is not strange that they have been the subject of so much study. Yet there is much about them that we do not know. Perhaps you will be the one to add to our knowledge. But even if you never lift a frame from a hive, or track a wild swarm to its hollow-tree home, what you have read about bees should make you a better citizen, for bees always work for the common good, cooperating in all their activities. Wisely they plan for the future, storing up treasure for themselves and their children. If each one of us would only copy their industry, display the same perseverance and patient skill when faced with a job to do and labor in equal harmony with our fellows, the *Wonders of the Hive* would not seem so remarkable.

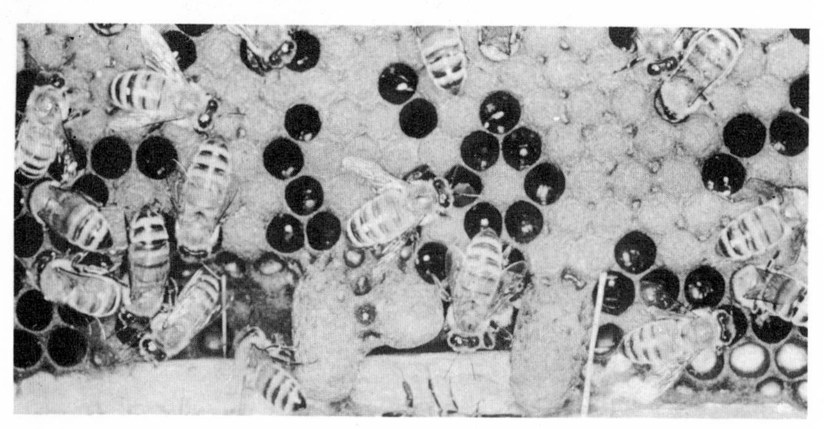

Photograph courtesy Ontario Agricultural College

Always working for the common good, bees teach the value of cooperation.

Index